Witness to History

The Vietnam War

Michael Burgan

Heinemann Library
Chicago, Illinois

© 2004 Heinemann Library
a division of Reed Elsevier Inc.
Chicago, Illinois

Customer Service 888-454-2279
Visit our website at www.heinemannlibrary.com

Produced for Heinemann by Discovery Books Ltd.
Photo Research by Rachel Tisdale
Originated by Ambassador Litho Ltd.
Printed and bound in Hong Kong, China by South
   China Printing Company

08 07 06 05 04
10 9 8 7 6 5 4 3 2 1

Library of Congress Cataloging-in-Publication Data
Cataloging-in-Publication data is on file at the Library of Congress.

Acknowledgments
The author and publishers are grateful to the following for permission to reproduce copyright material:
Bettmann/CORBIS pp. **8**, **12**, **14**, **17**, **18**, **19**, **20**, **21**, **24**, **26**, **32**, **34**, **35**, **36**, **40**, **42**, **48**; Bob Rowan; Progressive Image/CORBIS p. **47**; CORBIS SYGMA p. **33**; Francoise de Mulder/CORBIS p. **46**; Gideon Mendel/CORBIS p. **49**; Hulton-Deutsch Collection/CORBIS p.**7**; Nik Wheeler/CORBIS p. **44**; Peter Newark's Military Pictures p. **31**; Popperphoto pp. **25**, **38**, **51**; Steve Raymer/CORBIS p. **43**; Tim Page/CORBIS p. **28**; TophamPicturepoint pp. **4**, **5**, **10**, **16**, **22**.

Cover photograph shows a war photographer working alongside U.S. soldiers in South Vietnam recording his experiences, reproduced with permission of Bettmann/CORBIS.

The publisher would like to thank Bob Rees, historian and assistant head teacher, for his assistance in the preparation of this book.

Every effort has been made to contact copyright holders of any material reproduced in this book. Any omissions will be rectified in subsequent printings if notice is given to the publisher.

The paper used to print this book comes from sustainable resources.

Disclaimer
All Internet addresses (URLs) given in this book were valid at the time of going to press. However, due to the dynamic nature of the Internet, some addresses may have changed, or sites may have changed or ceased to exist since publication. While the author and publisher regret any inconvenience this may cause readers, no responsibility for any such changes can be accepted by either the author or the publisher.

Words appearing in the text in bold, **like this,** are explained in the glossary.

Contents

Introduction

For almost 30 years, the U.S. tried to influence events in Vietnam, a small Asian nation more than 7,000 miles (11,000 kilometers) from its Pacific coast. The U.S. interest in Vietnamese affairs led to the Vietnam War (1959-1975), one of the most devastating conflicts of the 20th century. The long war killed about one million soldiers, most of them Vietnamese. Several million civilians also died, and the fighting spread beyond Vietnam to the neighboring countries of Cambodia and Laos.

As the Vietnam War progressed, it led many Americans to question their government and its policies. Some people around the world said the war was immoral, since the U.S. was not directly threatened by Vietnam. They felt that a large, powerful nation was killing innocent people for its own selfish ends. Others, however, said the U.S. did have a valid reason for fighting in Vietnam: to stop the spread of what it considered to be an evil political system, **communism.**

Path to war

At the end of World War II (1939-1945), a group of Vietnamese communists led by Ho Chi Minh declared Vietnam's independence from France. The U.S. government gave France financial aid as it fought to keep control of Vietnam. This first Vietnam War ended in 1954, with Ho's victory forcing the French out of **Indochina.** The war, however, left Vietnam split. Ho and the communists controlled the north, while a pro-American, anti-communist government ruled the south. Ho, still seeking a unified Vietnam, aided communists in the south. These Vietnamese were known as the **Viet Cong.** In 1959, the North Vietnamese government officially approved using force in the south to achieve its political goals.

Wearing traditional peasant clothes, Viet Cong **guerrillas** search for enemy forces. Vietnam was largely a poor, agricultural country when the war began.

On a search-and-destroy mission, a U.S. soldier destroys a hut, part of a camp used by the Viet Cong.

The United States supported Ngo Dinh Diem, South Vietnam's leader at the time, sending him money, arms, and military advisors. Starting in 1961, President John F. Kennedy increased the number of advisors. About 16,000 served in Vietnam by the time of his **assassination** in November 1963. Less than two years later, President Lyndon Johnson sent the first U.S. combat troops to fight the Viet Cong and the North Vietnamese soldiers who were helping them. By 1969, more than 500,000 U.S. troops were fighting in Vietnam.

Starting in 1969, under President Richard Nixon, the U.S. pursued a new policy. Facing growing criticism of the war, Nixon pulled out U.S. troops while equipping its South Vietnamese **allies** so they could continue the fighting. Nixon also increased U.S. military activity in Laos and Cambodia, hoping to limit North Vietnamese activity in those countries. At the same time, the U.S. and North Vietnam held peace talks. In January 1973, the two sides reached an agreement, and the last U.S. combat troops soon left Vietnam. The war, however, continued for two more years—North Vietnam against South Vietnam. In the end, the North Vietnamese won, creating a single communist state.

How Do We Know?

The Vietnam War has been called a "television war." For the first time in history, people around the world could turn on their TV sets and see daily reports on the fighting. Some historians think that seeing the horrors of war so vividly while sitting in their homes increased the opposition of many Americans to the war. Vietnam also attracted international journalists and photographers who roamed the battlefields and villages, trying to uncover the truth about the fighting. About 75 journalists from all types of media died covering the Vietnam War.

Newspapers and television reports are two examples of primary sources. They provide direct evidence of what was said and done during the Vietnam War. Other primary sources include government documents, the later writings of government officials, and oral (spoken) histories—personal accounts from people who were there at the time. A number of oral histories provide the views of soldiers and civilians from both sides of the war.

Primary sources are used by historians and scholars to create secondary sources—books, articles, and documentaries that describe and interpret the war. Good secondary sources are factually accurate, but they still reflect the attitudes and beliefs of the people who create them. Sometimes a variety of primary and secondary sources, taken together, provide the most balanced view of a topic. Secondary sources are only as good as the primary sources they are based on, and a primary source might provide a distorted view of the truth. One person's experiences on a war front, for instance, gives only a small part of the overall picture. People speaking or writing long after the war might forget how something actually happened. Personal accounts are also colored by the opinions of the people recollecting events. The people involved might also lie about their actions, to cover up a mistake or take credit for something they did not do.

New sources emerge

Primary sources from governments provide useful information on official polices. Government sources, however, are no more objective than personal accounts. And at times, governments keep some information **classified.** This process prevents an enemy—or their own citizens—from learning the truth about sensitive issues. The U.S. government kept many documents classified during the Vietnam War. Over time, the government has **declassified** some of them, shedding new light on certain issues. New primary sources also come from Vietnam and its wartime **allies** the Soviet Union and China. In 1991, **communism** ended in the Soviet Union and the government was replaced. Afterward, new leaders allowed Western scholars to see some previously secret documents. The Chinese and Vietnamese have also opened up some of their **archives** because they have developed better relations with the **West.** Still, all the governments that took part in the war keep some documents classified. Scholars might need decades to uncover all the facts about the Vietnam War.

In 1968, war photographers Larry Burrows and Terry Fincher take a break from the action. Journalists from both print and electronic media gave the world detailed accounts of the Vietnam War. Burrows was killed covering a South Vietnamese offensive in 1971.

Colonial Vietnam

In 111 B.C.E., China invaded Vietnam. The Chinese ruled there for more than 1,000 years, until the mid-10th century, when the Vietnamese finally forced them out and established an independent kingdom. That independence lasted until 1862, when the Vietnamese emperor Tu Duc gave control of part of his country to France. In the 19th century, France, like other European nations, wanted **colonies** in Asia. The French slowly extended their control over the rest of Vietnam and neighboring Laos and Cambodia, creating what was called French **Indochina.**

Under French rule, Vietnamese **nationalism** began to develop. During the 1920s and 1930s, a young nationalist and **communist** named Ho Chi Minh led the resistance to the French. When World War II began, Japan invaded Vietnam. During the war, the French government came under German control, and it worked with the Japanese in Indochina. Ho decided the Vietnamese should fight both colonial powers: France and Japan. Ho and other communists formed the *Viet Nam Doc Lap Minh*—the Vietnam Independence League. Known as the Viet Minh, this group battled against the Japanese and the French throughout the war. On September 2, 1945, Japan surrendered to the U.S., Great Britain, and their **allies.** The same day, Ho Chi Minh announced the creation of a new independent country: the **Democratic Republic** of Vietnam.

In 1862, the French gained control of Cochin China, part of Vietnam. By 1893 they had taken over the whole region.

Ho Chi Minh founded Vietnam's Communist Party in 1930. He led the party until his death in 1969.

Declaration of independence

When he announced his country's independence, Ho Chi Minh deliberately drew on the wording of the American Declaration of Independence, in which the American colonies declared their independence from the British Empire. Here is part of his declaration of independence for Vietnam.

All men are created equal; they are endowed [given] by their Creator with certain unalienable Rights [rights that cannot be taken away]; among these are Life, Liberty, and the pursuit of Happiness.

This immortal [endlessly important] statement was made in the Declaration of Independence of the United States of America in 1776. In a broader sense, this means: All the peoples on the earth are equal from birth, all the peoples have a right to live, to be happy and free.

The Declaration of the French Revolution made in 1791 on the Rights of Man and the Citizen also states: "All men are born free and with equal rights, and must always remain free and have equal rights."

Those are undeniable truths.

*Nevertheless, for more than eighty years, the French **imperialists**, abusing the standard of Liberty, Equality, and Fraternity, have violated [treated with disrespect] our Fatherland and oppressed our fellow citizens. They have acted contrary to the ideals of humanity and justice ...*

After the Japanese had surrendered to the Allies, our whole people rose to regain our national sovereignty and to found the Democratic Republic of Viet-Nam...

The whole Vietnamese people, animated [made active] by a common purpose, are determined to fight to the bitter end against any attempt by the French colonialists to reconquer their country.

The French War

Around the world, many **colonized** people hoped the end of World War II would lead to their independence. France did grant independence to some of its former colonies, such as Syria and Lebanon, but French leaders considered **Indochina** too valuable to give up. They ignored Ho's declaration of independence, though they signed an agreement with the Viet Minh in March 1946 that would make Vietnam a so-called "free state" within France's empire. French troops would stay in Vietnam, although the Vietnamese would run the local government and have their own army. The two sides, however, began fighting before they worked out the details of this agreement.

In November 1946, Viet Minh and French forces clashed in Haiphong. The French then bombarded the city, killing more than 6,000 people. The next month, Ho's forces attacked the French, starting a war that would last for almost eight years. Ho had hoped the U.S. would recognize his country's independence. President Harry Truman, however, wanted to restore French rule in Vietnam. American leaders wanted French support for their international policies and they distrusted Ho's **communist** background.

Medical workers carry a French soldier wounded at Dien Bien Phu in May 1954. About 2,000 French troops were killed and thousands more were taken prisoner, out of a force of about 16,000.

Starting in 1950, the U.S. sent money and supplies to the French. By 1954, the Americans were paying for almost 80 percent of the war effort. Still, the Vietnamese fought on, and in May 1954 General Vo Nguyen Giap led them to victory at the battle of Dien Bien Phu. With their defeat, the French decided to pull out of Vietnam for good.

The battle at Dien Bien Phu was a six-week long **siege.** About 60,000 well-armed Viet Minh had taken control of the mountains surrounding the French camps there. In March 1954, they began to pound the French with **artillery** fire before finally taking control of the camps in May. Jean Pouget, a French soldier, describes his experience at Dien Bien Phu.

I arrived during the night of May 2, and Dien Bien Phu fell on May 7. The memory I keep of it is one block of time. There was no day or night. I never lay down. I never slept. I don't remember eating. At four o'clock in the morning there was a lull. We were 35 left at my post, with one machine gun, one grenade left . . . We built a barricade with corpses at the entrance since we had no sandbags, and we waited. And we saw the shadows coming one by one, the Viet Minh. I decided to throw my grenade and we immediately got return fire. One of my last impressions was to feel the wall of corpses shivering under the burst of fire. Then a grenade must have hit my helmet because the net was burned and the helmet dented. American helmets are very solid. I lost consciousness and when I came to, there was above me, very close, a surgeon's mask from which a voice came: "You are a prisoner of the army of the **Democratic Republic of Vietnam.**"

Cold War Conflict

The U.S. interest in **Indochina** was shaped by the **Cold War.** This **ideological** battle between the **democratic-capitalist** United States (and its **allies**) and the **communist** Soviet Union (and its allies) began after World War II. The Soviet Union wanted to extend its influence around the world by supporting communist governments that it could then control. The U.S. sought to promote capitalism and democratic governments, while halting Soviet gains.

In the 1950s, communism seemed to be spreading rapidly. In 1949, communists led by Mao Zedong had taken control of China. Mao had received some aid from the Soviet Union, though he and Soviet leaders sometimes disagreed. The next year, the Soviets backed an invasion of South Korea (an ally of the U.S.) by communist North Korea. This began the Korean War (1950-1953). These two events convinced U.S. leaders that the Soviet Union wanted to dominate Asia.

The military aid the U.S. gave France to fight the Viet Minh was part of the U.S. strategy of containment, or stopping the spread of communism. In 1954, President Dwight D. Eisenhower talked about the "domino theory:" if one South-east Asian nation came under communist control, its neighbors would too. The countries were like dominoes lined up in a row—when one fell, the others would fall after them. The U.S. was determined to prevent Vietnam from falling to communism.

John Foster Dulles, left, and President Dwight Eisenhower shaped early U.S. policies toward South-east Asia. Dulles served as U.S. secretary of state from 1953 to 1959.

Shaping U.S. policy

John Foster Dulles was President Eisenhower's secretary of state, advising him on foreign affairs. Dulles helped shape the U.S. policy on Vietnam. On March 29, 1954, about a month before the fall of Dien Bien Phu, Dulles suggested that the U.S. might have to play a direct military role in Indochina. Here is part of his speech.

Recent statements have been designed to impress upon potential aggressors that aggression might lead to action at places and by means of free-world choosing, so that aggression would cost more than it could gain.

. . . Under all circumstances it seems desirable to clarify further the United States' position.

Under the conditions of today, the imposition in South-east Asia of the political system of Communist Russia and its Chinese Communist ally, by whatever means, would be a grave threat to the whole free community. The United States feels that that possibility should not be passively accepted but should be met by united action. This might involve serious risks. But these risks are far less than those that will face us a few years from now if we dare not be resolute today.

The free nations want peace. However, peace is not had merely by wanting it. Peace has to be worked for and planned for. Sometimes it is necessary to take risks to win peace just as it is necessary in war to take risks to win victory. The chances for peace are usually bettered by letting a potential aggressor know in advance where his aggression could lead him.

Two Vietnams

During the summer of 1954, French and Viet Minh leaders met in Geneva, Switzerland, to officially end their war. Joining them at this conference were representatives from several other countries with an interest in finding peace and influencing events in **Indochina;** these included China, the Soviet Union, Great Britain, and the U.S. The agreement signed in Geneva split Vietnam at the **17th parallel** and created a **demilitarized zone** there. Ho and the Viet Minh controlled the country north of this line. In the south was the State of Vietnam, a pro-French, anti-**communist** government that opposed Ho. This situation was only meant to be temporary and, under the accords (agreements), all Vietnamese would choose the leaders of a unified government in 1956.

In 1954, Vietnam was divided into North and South at the 17th parallel. The map also shows important places mentioned in the book.

In the north, Ho began putting a communist system in place. His government killed many landowners and took their farms, a policy Viet Minh leaders later admitted was a mistake. Meanwhile, in the south, Ngo Dinh Diem emerged as the leader. Using violence and fraud, he won an election and founded the **Republic** of Vietnam (South Vietnam). Diem ignored the Geneva Conference's plans for nationwide elections. He was determined to rule a separate, non-communist Vietnam, and the U.S. openly supported him.

Viet Minh troops march into Hanoi after taking control of the city from the French in October 1954.

I was ten years old when a Viet Minh convinced me to go to a secret school . . . I just followed their instructions. They had me distribute handwritten leaflets around the marketplace saying things about higher salaries and justice. And they asked me to introduce them to three of my friends: "One becomes three; three becomes nine and this way we will have many people."

. . . My teacher told me, "Do you know why Ngo Dinh Diem came to Vietnam? He was sent by the U.S. Now his whole family has power and all the poor people must work to feed them. Who should run Vietnam—Diem or Ho Chi Minh?"

They never called themselves Communists during this time. But they said, "The Vietnamese people want to have a free government. Nothing is better than independence and liberty. Our best friend is the Soviet Union. It took the United States a hundred years to have progress but in only forty years the Soviet Union has become prosperous. Why? Because the Americans are capitalists, a few people take power. But in the Soviet Union the power is in the hands of all the people."

I said "That's wonderful. Really wonderful." And I tried to march along with them.

The Advisors

To protect his government, Ngo Dinh Diem arrested and sometimes killed the Viet Minh (members of the Vietnam Independence League) and their supporters in South Vietnam. In 1959, Ho decided the Viet Minh should fight back, and they began a **guerrilla war** against Diem's forces. The **communist** fighters in the south were called the **Viet Cong** (VC). The next year, the North Vietnamese organized the National Liberation Front (NLF) in South Vietnam. This political group included non-communists who opposed Diem, but Ho and his aides (assistants) directed it as they pursued their goal of unification.

In January 1961, John F. Kennedy replaced Dwight Eisenhower as president of the United States. Eisenhower had sent 900 U.S. military advisors to Vietnam to help Diem fight the Viet Cong. The advisors included U.S. Special Forces—troops trained to fight with great secrecy behind enemy lines. The U.S. was also providing economic aid (money) to the South Vietnamese army, the ARVN (Army of the **Republic** of Vietnam). Kennedy, concerned about growing communist influence around the world, decided to increase the U.S. commitment to South Vietnam. The president sent more money. He also sent helicopters and aircraft. U.S. advisors flew these aircraft and sometimes helped the ARVN fight the Viet Cong. In public, however, the government downplayed the role U.S. soldiers played in Vietnam and kept secret some of their activities.

The North Vietnamese and Viet Cong often made the rockets and shells they fired at the ARVN and U.S. troops by hand.

New York Times

Today American warships are helping the Vietnamese Navy to guard the sea frontier against infiltration from North Vietnam and U.S. Navy servicemen presently will arrive to help clean out guerrillas from the maze of tidal waterways in the Mekong River delta. The U.S. Army helicopter crews have come under fire taking Vietnamese combat troops into guerrilla zones or carrying pigs and other livestock to hungry outposts surrounded by hostile country. U.S. Air Force pilots have flown with Vietnamese pilots on bombing missions against reported enemy concentrations and against two frontier forts recently evacuated by the Vietnamese Army.

So far our contribution in blood has been small. One American sergeant has been killed by enemy action and another is missing and presumed captured. Inevitably, our casualties will grow.

. . . The United States seems . . . committed to a long, inconclusive war. The Communists can prolong it for years. Even without large-scale interventions from the North . . . what may be achieved at best is only a restoration of a tolerable security . . . But it is too late to disengage [pull out]; our prestige has been committed. Washington says we will stay until the finish.

In October 1963, a U.S. military advisor watches as two South Vietnamese troops set up their weapon. That year, a U.S. government report claimed the Americans and South Vietnamese were winning the war.

Widening the War

The **assassination** of John F. Kennedy on November 22, 1963, thrust Vice President Lyndon B. Johnson into the White House. LBJ, as he was called, kept Kennedy's aides (advisors) and the commitment to prevent a **communist** takeover in South Vietnam. The war seemed to be going poorly. At times, U.S. generals considered the use of **nuclear weapons** against North Vietnam. Some also suggested conventional bombing there and along the **Viet Cong** supply route from the north called the Ho Chi Minh Trail, which ran through parts of Cambodia and Laos. Johnson, however, was reluctant to pursue open, direct military involvement.

LBJ changed his mind in August 1964. That month, a U.S. spy ship briefly came under attack in the Gulf of Tonkin, off the coast of North Vietnam. The U.S. government later wrongly claimed that the North Vietnamese attacked a second time, and Johnson used that claim to put the Tonkin Gulf Resolution before **Congress.** If approved, this would give the president further powers to wage a wider war against North Vietnam. Congress did approve it.

By this time the U.S. military was already carrying out secret missions in North Vietnam, blowing up bridges and other important targets. U.S. planes were also bombing Viet Cong positions in Laos, along Vietnam's western border. The North Vietnamese had set up training camps there. Johnson soon ordered massive bombing raids on the North Vietnamese capital, Hanoi. And on March 8, 1965, the first 3,500 U.S. combat troops arrived in South Vietnam. The number grew to more than 180,000 by the end of 1965.

Lyndon Johnson was determined to stop the spread of communism, yet he was reluctant at first to increase the U.S. military presence in South-east Asia.

U.S. troops fought one of their first major ground battles of the Vietnam War at Ia Drang. The enemy included both Viet Cong and members of the North Vietnamese Army (NVA). Jack Smith was a private first class with the U.S. 7th Cavalry. Here he recounts some of the sights and sounds of battle.

Nothing prepares you for combat. The best way to prepare a company for combat is to line the company up against a wall and fire a machine gun at them for about ten seconds. And tell the survivors, "You're now combat-trained." That's not pleasant, but that's what combat's like.

We walked in and we got into Landing Zone X-Ray on the third day of the battle there. It was just about over . . . I had never seen men as filthy as that . . . Their clothing was so covered with dirt, they looked like they were part of the dirt because they had been living in the dirt, living in foxholes for three days. They all had these thousand-yard stares that people talk about. The stare of someone who is nineteen years old but going on fifty, who has seen combat and been killing people and seen his friends killed under continuous bombardment, artillery and **napalm**, day in, day out. Stacks of dead bodies, stacks of wounded, equipment around the landing zone. And the one thing that sticks in my mind, there were bullets whizzing over the landing zone, humming like bees.

U.S. Marines land at Da Nang, South Vietnam, in March 1965, as the U.S. commits itself to a full-scale war.

19

Friend or Foe?

The **Viet Cong** (VC) used a variety of tactics to fight their **guerrilla war.** They hid in the rain forests and swamps, waiting to **ambush** enemy troops. They built simple traps in the ground filled with sharp sticks, called *punjis*, which were often tipped with poison. For weapons, the VC used captured U.S. guns as well as arms sent from the Soviet Union and China. As the war went on, they also relied on military help from the North Vietnamese Army (NVA). Starting in 1964, these regular troops fought side-by-side with the VC.

A U.S. soldier walks carefully through bamboo *punji* sticks in November 1965. Viet Cong booby traps such as these struck about 28 percent of the U.S. forces killed or injured during combat.

From the beginning of the Vietnam War, U.S. troops struggled to distinguish the Viet Cong and their supporters from ordinary civilians. Viet Cong dressed as typical peasants and lived and worked in the villages the Americans patrolled. If U.S. troops searched a village, the fighters fled, hiding in nearby rain forest or fields. The VC returned when the Americans left. U.S. troops sometimes destroyed villages where suspected VC lived. Innocent people lost their homes—and sometimes their lives—in these raids. The Americans, however, felt they could not take chances, since many civilians were fighting for the Viet Cong. U.S. soldiers could never be sure if the people they met had a bomb strapped to their body or a gun hidden in a farm cart.

Very few people betrayed us. That's why the Americans killed civilians . . .

Civilians were put in concentration camps . . . At night nobody was permitted to leave the camps. In the daytime, if the soldiers didn't think the people were going to help the Viet Cong, they let them go to the fields, to let them grow rice, potato, manioc.

When entering South Vietnamese villages, U.S. troops often had trouble telling friend from foe because Viet Cong guerrillas dressed as civilians.

. . . We had no weapons. The Americans and their coalition [allies] had very modern weapons — simple against modern, so we had to be clever. They didn't know that the VC surrounded their camps. We took unexploded bombs and shells, and made mines. We put them on the roads and destroyed their tanks. We saw where they were coming and mined those places . . . We made a huge mine, took a 200-liter can of petrol [gas], filled it with explosives, connected it to a line and planted it on [a] hill . . . We saw a lot of smoke and American bodies flying in the air, and then we heard the explosion. Helicopters came and removed the bodies, but they left one. We bound him in cloth and buried him. Alive they were our enemies, but in death we were all human.

Methods of War

The U.S. often changed its strategy and tactics during the war. At first, the U.S. strengthened South Vietnam's defenses, to prevent a possible attack from the north. Then, the Americans and South Vietnamese adapted to the **Viet Cong**'s **guerrilla warfare.** Part of their new strategy included building "strategic hamlets." Civilians were placed in guarded **stockades** so they could not aid the Viet Cong. But, the people hated being forced from their homes, so the program was dropped.

When U.S. ground troops arrived, they used a tactic called "search and destroy." They hunted for VC camps and destroyed them or tried to catch the enemy in an **ambush.** The Viet Cong, however, were often able to slip away before the Americans could reach them. Against the NVA, U.S. forces used **artillery** and received air support from planes and helicopters. The Americans also dropped chemicals such as Agent Orange. This **defoliant** killed trees and plants that the VC and NVA used to hide their movements. However, it also had side effects that still affect people today.

The U.S. hoped massive bombing attacks in the north would break North Vietnam's will to continue the war. Using its huge B-52 bombers and other planes, the U.S. military dropped more bombs during this war than both sides used during World War II.

Huge clouds of flames mark a napalm attack. Both sides used the chemical. The North Vietnamese fired it from handheld weapons called flamethrowers, while the Americans dropped it as bombs from aircraft.

Report from an anti-war conference

In Vietnam, U.S. planes often dropped **napalm** on their enemy. In 1971, panelists at an anti-war conference in Detroit, Michigan, described the impact of napalm on its victims.

PANELIST: In Dong Ha, located about 18 miles south of the **demilitarized zone**, they have a children's hospital. It's all Vietnamese children . . . They had a lot of children in there for treatment of diseases. There was one specific child I saw. I asked the child what had happened to him, and he said he'd been hit by napalm. His face, from his right eye around the back of his head (and had no ear), on down to the middle of his chest, was like one big mass of scar that'd just grown together. He'd been treated, but there's not a whole lot they can do for him. There's several of these cases, you know. I'm sure these people could tell you.

MODERATOR: Who else saw it? Anybody else see napalm?

DR. DAVID GALICIA: I saw the effects a couple of times. One I distinctly remember was a lady I used to see out in the yard in between two of the wards. This lady'd been burned beyond recognition, facial-wise. She had no face. Her eyes were left and they had somehow or another grafted some skin over the front of her head. She had some sort of an orifice left that she could take food through, but that's about it. She'd been the victim of napalm.

The South Vietnamese

The Vietnam War drastically changed daily life for the South Vietnamese—usually for the worse. A few people, particularly Buddhist monks, tried to protest against the war. Buddhists were a majority of the population in South Vietnam, but the country's leaders were Roman Catholics and denied them political power.

The largely Catholic government had many **corrupt** leaders. At times, they stole U.S. aid meant to strengthen the military and the country's economy. South Vietnam never developed a true **democratic** government, despite holding elections during the mid-1960s.

The war had perhaps its greatest impact on the peasants of South Vietnam. To escape the fighting, thousands of rural South Vietnamese fled to the cities, where they lived in poverty. Those who stayed in their villages had to deal with the Viet Cong, who sometimes forced the peasants to provide food or hiding places. Some people, however, welcomed the Viet Cong, even though they had to pay them taxes and sacrifice some of their freedom. The **communists** seemed to offer more hope for a better future than their own corrupt leaders. And while the Americans talked of winning the "hearts and minds" of the South Vietnamese, some U.S. troops held racist attitudes toward them. They insulted the South Vietnamese, calling them "gooks" and "slopes" while raiding their villages and sometimes killing innocent people.

Buddhist monks demonstrating in Saigon, capital of South Vietnam, in 1966, demand the resignation of the president, Nguyen Van Thieu.

Coping with the Americans

Le Ly Hayslip was 12 years old when U.S. troops first arrived in her village of Ky La, South Vietnam. In her autobiography *When Heaven and Earth Changed Places,* Hayslip described how she and her friends reacted to the Americans.

In time, we all would learn the wisdom of standing still at the approach of Americans— the way one learns to stand still in the face of an angry dog. Before long, any Vietnamese who ran from American gunships would be considered Viet Cong and shot down for the crime of fear.

In 1966, a U.S. marine visits a school in Da Nang, part of an American effort to win the support of South Vietnamese civilians.

Although Americans had been in the village before and now came more frequently to Ky La, we children never got used to them. Because they had blue eyes and always wore sunglasses, a few of us thought they were blind. We called them mat meo—cat eyes—and "long nose" to their backs and repeated every wild story we heard about them. Because the Viet Cong, when they captured them, always removed the Americans' boots (making escape too painful for their soft, citified feet), we thought we could immobilize the Americans by stealing both their sunglasses and their shoes. How can a soldier fight, we reasoned, if he's not only blind but lame?

Still, the arrival of the Americans in ever-increasing numbers meant the new war had expanded beyond anyone's wildest dreams. A period of great danger—one we couldn't imagine at the time—was about to begin.

Life During Wartime

In North Vietnam, the people were united behind Ho Chi Minh, who was sometimes called "Uncle Ho." This was because most Northerners who opposed **communism** had already fled the country, been imprisoned, or been killed. The Communist Party controlled everything in the north, and citizens had to join if they wanted good jobs. Peasants and young soldiers learned communist philosophy, and North Vietnamese leaders stressed that the war was meant to free the south from American **imperialism.** Still, as the deaths mounted, some North Vietnamese did question the war, though rarely in public. Some young men tried to avoid the **draft**—just as many young Americans did.

U.S. bombings disrupted life in the north. Food was scarce, and schools, factories, and stores had to move from the cities to the countryside to escape the bombs. Civilians built bunkers, where they could seek protection during the raids. Hundreds of thousands of North Vietnamese also helped build and maintain the Ho Chi Minh Trail. Using mostly shovels and their hands, the North Vietnamese turned a simple rain forest path into a major supply highway. The trail had several different routes that stretched for a total of almost 10,000 miles (16,000 kilometers).

The North Vietnamese used their own bicycles and Soviet-made trucks to move supplies along the Ho Chi Minh Trail.

During the bombings everyone suffered. Hatred for Saigon [the South Vietnamese capital] and the Americans grew even stronger than it had before. A lot of young people volunteered for the army at that time.

But there was also a lot of anxiety. Everybody was excited by news about our great victories in the South and about the opposition movements that were fighting against the inhuman regime in Saigon. But there was no news from my friends who had gone South—nobody was hearing anything . . . So there was a lot of confusion about what was really going on and a lot of tension. When people would complain or ask questions they were criticized or arrested by the security police . . .

Nobody could get away from the war. It didn't matter if you were in the countryside or the city. While I was living in the country I saw terrible things . . . I saw children who had been killed, pagodas [Buddhist temples] and churches that had been destroyed, monks and priests dead in the ruins, schoolboys who were killed when their schools were bombed. When I saw these horrors my only feeling was that I wanted to kill Americans.

The Media War

Reporters from around the world tried to capture the reality of the Vietnam War. As during past wars, print journalists covered battles and analyzed the progress of the war. But for the first time ever, television also played a major part in reporting a foreign war. At first, U.S. television networks limited their broadcast of combat scenes. Still, what they did show upset some U.S. officials, who wanted to **censor** the television reporting. The images, they feared, would weaken public support for the war, and some historians say the broadcasts did have that effect.

A CBS camera crew interviews American soldiers on Tay Ninh Road. The U.S. government often disliked the American media's coverage of the war in Vietnam.

The journalists argued that they merely reported what they saw and heard—and told the truth when the government did not. Some journalists were openly against the war. Others began to oppose it only after seeing civilians killed or coming to the conclusion that the war could not be won. During the 1960s, Walter Cronkite was one of the most respected TV news figures in America. In 1968, he began to question the war. President Johnson realized that if Cronkite no longer supported him, many average Americans must feel the same way.

Reporting the war
Western reporters often attended **press conferences,** held
in Saigon. Some of the journalists distrusted what they
learned and called the daily reports "the 5 o'clock Follies."
Richard Pyle, an American reporter for the Associated Press,
describes the "Follies" and his experience in Vietnam.

These briefings were much ridiculed, and there
were many valid criticisms. But . . . for all
their failings, the Follies were not the pack
of lies that some critics suggested. The best
reporters and news organizations recognized the
value of an on-the-record, official version of
events to compare with information from field
reporters and other sources.

As important as it was to get the official
version, there was no substitute for hands-on
coverage, and reporters and photographers were
always in the field. We drove down roads until
the emptiness told us not to go any further.
We trudged and sweated with the infantry and
Marines, made harrowing helicopter assaults
into landing zones, cowered behind paddy dikes
as bullets cracked overhead. We waited long
hours at isolated helicopter pads, saw B-52
strikes blossom like giant brown flowers,
learned the culinary tricks of a C-ration [food
for soldiers in the field], interviewed
generals, lieutenants, sergeants and privates
in their natural habitat, where the truth at
least was bullet-proof.

Field officers and soldiers welcomed
journalists; they wanted people at home to
know what they were doing and enduring, and
recognized our readiness to share their perils
to tell their story.

Trouble at Home

The **civil rights** movement was under way as the Vietnam War began. The movement's goal was to win legal equality for African-Americans. Civil rights leader Martin Luther King also spoke out against the war. He realized that the more money the U.S. government spent on the war, the less it could spend to help poor people, which included many African-Americans. King also saw that a higher percentage of blacks and other minorities were serving on the front lines in Vietnam, compared to the percentage of **draft-**age whites. For the first years of the war, young men in college, who were more likely to be white, had received deferments, meaning they were not eligible for the draft.

As more Americans began to oppose the war, they adopted some of the methods of the civil rights movement, such as marches and non-violent **demonstrations.** The largest rallies drew hundreds of thousands of people. Some young men became draft-dodgers—they refused to report when chosen for military service. One of these was Muhammed Ali, the world heavyweight boxing champion who, because of his action, was stripped of his title. Such a famous name made people all over the world aware of the growing opposition to the war. Both President Johnson and Richard Nixon, who took over the presidency in 1969, thought the protesters were disloyal to their government.

The anti-war movement influenced popular culture. Musical groups sang songs against the war, and symbols of peace, such as two fingers raised in a V, appeared on posters and buttons. During past wars, the U.S. film industry had made movies that promoted the war effort. With rare exceptions, such as *The Green Berets,* starring John Wayne, film companies avoided making movies about Vietnam. They saw how split Americans were over fighting the war.

In 1917, Uncle Sam, a symbol of the United States, appeared on posters calling on Americans to help fight World War I with the slogan "I Want You." In 1971, Vietnam War protesters created this poster, showing a war-weary Sam with a different slogan.

An ex-soldier protests

Some soldiers returned from Vietnam thinking the U.S. government had made a mistake by entering the war. In 1967, a group of them formed Vietnam Veterans Against the War (VVAW). Ron Kovic, who lost the use of his legs in Vietnam, joined VVAW. Here is a selection from his autobiography, *Born on the Fourth of July*.

I was in Vietnam when I first heard about the thousands of people protesting the war in the streets of America. I didn't want to believe it at first—people protesting against us when we were putting our lives on the line for our country. The men in my outfit used to talk about it a lot. How could they do this to us? . . .

But the hospital had changed all that. It was the end of whatever belief I'd still had in what I'd done in Vietnam. Now I wanted to know what I had lost my legs for, why I and the others had gone at all. But it was still very hard for me to think of speaking out against the war, to think of joining those I'd once called traitors . . .

I WANT OUT

. . .There was going to be a march and a demonstration. I thought carefully for a moment or two, then decided to participate, driving my car past the hundreds of students marching down to the big parking lot where the rally was to be held . . . I stayed in my car during the rally, listening intently to each speaker and cheering and shouting with the crowd.

The POWs

As in other conflicts, both sides took prisoners of war (POWs). The South Vietnamese held both **Viet Cong** and NVA troops, while the **communists** took ARVN and Americans as prisoners. In the U.S., naturally, the media and the government focused on U.S. POWs as well as troops listed as missing in action (MIA).

The first U.S. POWs were members of the Special Forces, the advisors sent to aid the South Vietnamese. Later, air force and navy pilots shot down over North Vietnam made up the bulk of the POWs. Often found by hostile civilians, many of the pilots went to a Hanoi prison. The Americans nicknamed it "the Hanoi Hilton," after the famous hotel chain. About 800 Americans were taken as POWs, while almost 2,000 more were MIA.

Life as a POW

John McCain was a U.S. Navy pilot taken prisoner in 1967. He was held as a POW for more than five years. Later, he entered politics and served as a U.S. senator. He also ran for president in the 2000 election. In this interview, he describes some of his experiences as a POW.

A 1949 international agreement called the Geneva Convention outlined the treatment POWs should receive in captivity. North Vietnam had signed the agreement, but it ignored many of its requirements. (The South Vietnamese did as well.) The North Vietnamese and the Viet Cong often tortured American POWs or forced them to stay in tiny bamboo cages. The communists also used them for their **propaganda,** to try to convince their own people and foreigners that they were winning the war.

A young North Vietnamese woman points a gun at a U.S. pilot shot down near Hanoi in 1967. Most American POWs were captured pilots.

A group of Vietnamese . . . pulled me into shore. The crowd was very hostile. They began kicking and beating me . . . It was pretty tense and the army people came up, put me into a truck, took me to the Hanoi Hilton. I was in very bad shape so it didn't take a lot of interrogating. They would slap me a few times and I would go in and out of consciousness. But it was clear to me that they didn't provide medical treatment unless we gave military information.

I was on the floor of the cell for about four or five days with a blanket over me. One day the guard came in with one of his friends, pulled the blanket up. My knee was the size and shape and color of a football. I told him, I said, "Get the interrogator." The interrogator came in and I said, "Look, take me to the hospital, give me some treatment and then maybe we can talk about military information." . . . Some hours later . . . the door opened and the interrogator said, "Your father is a big admiral and we're going to take you to the hospital." So the fact that my father was an admiral in the navy saved my life.

President Richard Nixon greets former POW John McCain after his release from North Vietnam in 1973, after five and a half years in captivity.

Turning Points

By the end of 1967, President Lyndon Johnson faced heavy criticism for the war in Vietnam. The president's problems increased after January 30, 1968, when the **communists** launched the **Tet** offensive. Using hidden weapons and fighters, they launched a series of surprise attacks in South Vietnamese cities. Thousands of South Vietnamese civilians were massacred, including 2,800 in the city of Hue. The **Viet Cong** and NVA themselves lost thousands of their best troops. Tet, however, had a positive result for the north. More Americans now sensed that the U.S. was losing the war, even though U.S. officials had been telling them the opposite. Johnson's support fell even more, and in March he decided not to seek re-election.

A few months after Tet, U.S. troops raided the village of My Lai, looking for Viet Cong. Without being fired on, the soldiers massacred more than 400 civilians—women, children, and old men. The U.S. government tried to keep the attack secret, but in 1969, Americans learned about the "My Lai Massacre." Many were horrified about U.S. soldiers acting so cruelly. A commander on the scene that day, Lieutenant William Calley, was later **court-martialed** for killing 22 civilians. My Lai became a symbol for all that was wrong about the Vietnam War.

This scene shows the once-beautiful, ancient city of Hue. About 70 percent of the houses were destroyed during the communist Tet offensive in 1968. Thousands of civilians were killed.

Choosing not to kill

Hugh Thompson Jr. was a helicopter pilot at My Lai who tried to stop some of the killing. In 1998, in a computer chat session with the Cable News Network (CNN), he described his actions during the massacre.

It was clear to us that something was going wrong. And at one time we had asked for assistance on a wounded civilian and a captain walked up and shot the girl we'd asked assistance for. Another time, we'd seen an irrigation ditch full of bodies, of which some were still living. We landed and talked to the Americans on the ground, said there are some wounded civilians in the ditch, can you help them out. And we were told, yes, we'll help them out of their misery. I said, quit joking, how 'bout helping them, and they said OK. As I took off, they walked to the ditch, and we heard machine-gun fire . . . . Shortly after then, we saw some Vietnamese who had just made it to a bunker and were hiding inside the bunker. On the other side of the opening, we saw the American forces coming toward them. We just kind of figured those people were dead in about 15 seconds if we didn't do something. That's when we elected to land the aircraft between the American forces and the bunker . . . The things that went wrong that day were poor leadership, peer pressure and prejudice.

In 1971, Lt. William Calley (center) was sentenced to life in prison for his role in the My Lai Massacre. This sentence was later reduced to ten years; he served one-third of this time before winning his release.

Nixon's War

Just before the 1968 presidential election, Lyndon Johnson almost worked out a deal with North Vietnam to end the war—until South Vietnamese leader Nguyen Van Thieu refused to go along. Thieu had been in contact with representatives of Richard Nixon, the Republican candidate. Nixon encouraged Thieu to wait, saying he would offer better peace terms to South Vietnam if he were elected.

Nixon did win, and he promised Americans a new approach to defeating the **communists** in Vietnam and ending U.S. involvement. He began a policy called Vietnamization: the U.S. sent more military aid (money and weapons, backed by U.S. air power) to South Vietnam, so their own troops could do more of the fighting. At the same time, he began bringing home U.S. forces.

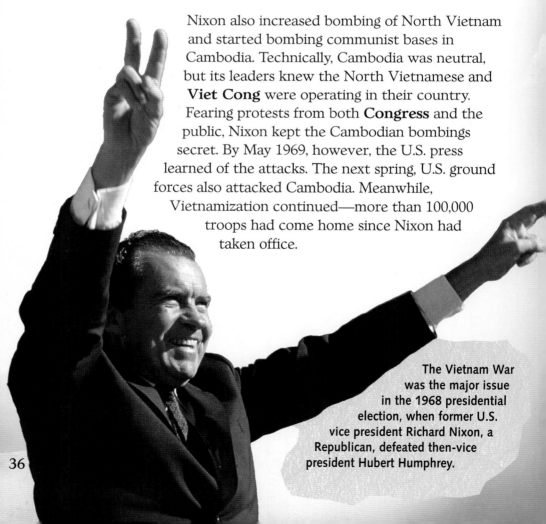

Nixon also increased bombing of North Vietnam and started bombing communist bases in Cambodia. Technically, Cambodia was neutral, but its leaders knew the North Vietnamese and **Viet Cong** were operating in their country. Fearing protests from both **Congress** and the public, Nixon kept the Cambodian bombings secret. By May 1969, however, the U.S. press learned of the attacks. The next spring, U.S. ground forces also attacked Cambodia. Meanwhile, Vietnamization continued—more than 100,000 troops had come home since Nixon had taken office.

The Vietnam War was the major issue in the 1968 presidential election, when former U.S. vice president Richard Nixon, a Republican, defeated then-vice president Hubert Humphrey.

This is not an invasion of Cambodia. The areas in which these attacks will be launched are completely occupied and controlled by North Vietnamese forces. Our purpose is not to occupy the areas. Once enemy forces are driven out of these sanctuaries and once their military supplies are destroyed, we will withdraw . . .

Now, let me give you the reasons for my decision.

A majority of the American people, a majority of you listening to me, are for the withdrawal of our forces from Vietnam. The action I have taken tonight is indispensable for the continuing success of that withdrawal program . . .

We take this action not for the purpose of expanding the war into Cambodia, but for the purpose of ending the war in Vietnam and winning the just peace we all desire. We have made and we will continue to make every possible effort to end this war through negotiation at the conference table rather than through more fighting on the battlefield . . .

If, when the chips are down, the world's most powerful nation, the United States of America, acts like a pitiful, helpless giant, the forces of totalitarianism and anarchy [absence of government] will threaten free nations and free institutions throughout the world.

A Distracted President

In the U.S., new **demonstrations** followed the invasion of Cambodia. On May 4, 1970, at Kent State University in Ohio, National Guard troops killed four students, which led to even greater protests. The next year, Nixon faced a new problem at home: the release of the Pentagon Papers. This massive set of documents traced the history of the U.S. role in **Indochina** from the end of World War II to 1968. The papers were never supposed to be made public, but Daniel Ellsberg, who worked at the Pentagon, gave them to reporters. Nixon was furious. Even though the Pentagon Papers dealt with policies shaped before he became president, Nixon did not want Americans to know the government had sometimes lied about its activities in Vietnam. He feared the public might question his own statements and actions.

On May 4, 1970, protestors at Kent State flee as troops open fire, killing four people. At a demonstration at Jackson State, an African-American college in Mississippi, two more students were killed.

Nixon ordered his staff to investigate Ellsberg. The staff also made a long list of "enemies"—celebrities and reporters who opposed Nixon and his policies. In 1972, the team in charge of these efforts ordered a secret burglary at the headquarters of the Democratic Party, the main rival of Nixon's Republican Party. The break-in took place at a Washington office complex called Watergate. Nixon began to focus more energy on trying to distance himself from the break-in and other illegal activities. The Watergate affair turned into the worst political scandal in U.S. history and it eventually forced Nixon to resign in 1974.

Lies and secrets

Bob Haldeman worked as one of Richard Nixon's top aides. His diary gives us an insight into the president's response to the *New York Times*' printing of the Pentagon Papers in June 1971. Nixon lost his legal challenge to stop the *Times* from printing all of the papers.

Tuesday, June 15, 1971

The big thing today was still the *New York Times* story follow-up, as they go on running it and the whole thing builds. [U.S. Attorney General John] Mitchell went ahead last night with his request of them to cease publication; they refused . . . After meeting with the P [Nixon] this afternoon, decided to file criminal charges. So we're pretty much in the soup on the whole thing now. The real problem is to try to establish clearly that the Administration's interest here is in the violation of Top Secret classifications rather than in the release of this particular material. The problem otherwise is that we're going to get tied into it and get blamed for the same kind of deception that was practiced by the Johnson Administration.

The P dictated a memo to me this morning, issuing orders that there is to be no contact . . . with the *New York Times* unless there is express permission from the P, which he does not intend to grant . . . He also felt that we should launch an attack on the *Times*; that it was a reckless disclosure of secrets and a shocking breach of security.

Talk of Peace

Nixon's key aide on foreign relations was national security advisor Henry Kissinger. Starting in 1970, Kissinger held secret talks with both China and the Soviet Union, hoping to improve relations with those two **communist** nations. Nixon made historic trips to both countries in 1972, and the Soviets and the Chinese began to press the North Vietnamese to end the war.

The most productive peace talks began in September 1972. Kissinger met Le Duc Tho, a North Vietnamese **diplomat,** in Paris. The U.S. promised to leave **Indochina.** Thieu would remain president of South Vietnam and continue to receive U.S. aid. The **Viet Cong** would also be allowed to stay in the south, and communists would have a role in the government there. For a while the talks broke down, and at Christmas, 1972, Nixon ordered the largest bombing raids of the war against North Vietnam. When the raids ended, the two sides agreed to the same terms they had reached earlier. Now, however, Thieu refused to accept the terms. With the threat of losing all U.S. aid, Thieu finally gave in, accepting the presence of communists in the South. Nixon proclaimed that the U.S. had achieved "peace with honor."

The Nixon Administration entered office determined to end our involvement in Vietnam. But it soon came up against the reality that had also bedeviled [been a problem for] its predecessor. For nearly a generation the security and progress of a free people [the South Vietnamese] had depended on confidence in America. We could not simply walk away from an enterprise [the war] involving two administrations, five allied countries, and thirty-one thousand dead as if we were switching a television channel . . .

The domestic turmoil [agitation within the U.S.] of the Vietnam debate therefore pained me deeply. I did not agree with many of the decisions that had brought about the impasse [deadlock] in Indochina; I felt, however, that my appointment to high office entailed [included] a responsibility to help end the war in a way compatible with American self-respect and the stake that all men and women of goodwill had in America's strength and purpose. It seemed to me important for America not to be humiliated, not to be shattered, but to leave Vietnam in a manner that even the protesters might later see as reflecting an American choice made with dignity and self-respect . . . it was precisely the issue of our self-confidence and faith in our future that I considered at stake in the outcome in Vietnam.

An interpreter stands between Henry Kissinger (left) and Le Duc Tho (right) who worked out the agreement that ended the U.S. involvement in the Vietnam War. The men shared the 1973 Nobel Peace Prize, which Tho rejected because his country was still at war.

Coming Home

Many U.S. soldiers had trouble adjusting to life at home when they returned from Vietnam. After past wars, returning U.S. troops were treated as heroes. While some Americans did honor the returning veterans, anti-war protesters sometimes spat on them or called them "babykillers." Some of the soldiers also returned home with wounds that left them permanently disabled. Others had emotional scars. Over time, doctors discovered that many veterans had post-**traumatic** stress disorder (PTSD). After seeing friends killed and having killed enemy troops or Vietnamese civilians, some soldiers suffered from recurring nightmares, depression, and physical ailments. Some veterans also came home addicted to drugs they had first used in Vietnam to escape the pressures of the war.

Good for some
Jim Noonan fought in Vietnam from September 1966 to October 1967. Unlike some veterans, he saw his experience in Vietnam as a positive influence on his life.

Vietnam veterans sometimes resented the treatment they received. Even after the last U.S. troops left Vietnam in March 1973, many Americans felt guilty about the U.S. role in **Indochina.** In 1982, however, the U.S. finally honored the veterans, with the Vietnam Veterans Memorial in Washington, D.C. A V-shaped granite wall features the names of all 58,229 American men and women killed during the Vietnam War.

At a 1970 rally, construction workers show their continuing support for the Vietnam War and the soldiers fighting it. By this time, widespread American support for the war had declined sharply.

I believed that it was my duty to go to Vietnam. And that has to do with the values my parents instilled in me. I'd like to think that I have maintained those values, because they are good ones. I'm very proud of my family. They're all honest, hardworking, caring people who would go out of their way for another human being if it would help that person. Of those values that I see as my best points now, Vietnam was part of their forming stages.

I got through high school by the skin of my teeth. But after Vietnam, I went through college in three years on the dean's list [list of exceptional students]. Yet, it's hard to reflect upon a situation where so many have suffered and think about it in terms of what you personally have gained. But I do think that as a result of my military experience I am a stronger and more confident person. I also doubt that I'll ever be that scared again. I can always think, "No matter what comes up, I'll know I've been more scared."

. . . in Vietnam, there were a lot of guys who put their life on the line for their brothers, for principle, for whatever reasons they thought it was important. And it's in the moment when a person makes that decision that the effort really stands out.

The Fall of Saigon

Under the 1973 peace treaty, North and South Vietnam agreed to a ceasefire. But the fighting soon resumed because the North Vietnamese had no intention of giving up their fight to control the South. And until August 1973, the U.S. continued to bomb **communist** bases in Cambodia. During that summer, **Congress** decided that the U.S. government would not spend more money to fight anywhere in **Indochina.** The U.S. as a whole was tired of the war and increasingly critical of Nixon, because of Watergate.

The **Viet Cong** slowly began to capture land under South Vietnamese government control. At the same time, South Vietnam faced economic troubles. The **refugees** in the cities lacked jobs and soldiers were going unpaid, while Thieu and his friends made money from **corruption.** The problems increased in 1974, when Congress cut $300 million from the money Nixon had promised Thieu.

In January 1975, the communists began their last major military campaign of the war. Within four months, they captured Saigon and took control of the South Vietnamese government. By this time, Cambodia was also ruled by local communists, and before the year's end Laos was under communist control as well. The U.S. policy of containment had failed in Indochina.

South Vietnam refugees move south toward Saigon to escape the last communist assault.

Life after war

The North Vietnamese and Viet Cong celebrated the end of the war. Southerners, however, faced new difficulties. Thieu's corrupt government was replaced by communist leaders who often used brutal tactics to ensure loyalty to their cause. Tran Van Luu, who later left Vietnam, describes life during peacetime in Saigon.

On April 30, 1975, as the Communists took over Saigon, my neighbors were just wandering in the streets, very shocked. Crowds mutely stared at tanks rolling by, carrying militia wearing red armbands and shooting into the air. We did not know what to do . . .

At first people came into the streets to watch the North Vietnamese fighters out of curiosity. There was no voluntary **demonstration** to support the new government. We regarded the Communists as strangers, not heroes. But after a few weeks, when the Communists organized demonstrations, a lot of people came because we were scared.

After the collapse, I chose to remain in Saigon. My wife was teaching school and I had enough money saved to buy and sell things. But I became more and more afraid for my family because there were public executions. The Communists appointed a very tough major to maintain order. I saw with my own eyes people being executed near the theater on Truong Minh Giang Street, where I lived. In front of a crowd of people, including children, they shot a young boy, just twelve or thirteen years old . . .

For my wife and children, the school system changed drastically. Teachers identified as having commitment to the former **republic** were arrested. The Communist Party sent in new teachers from the North to take over the schools in Saigon . . . Arithmetic was formed around such destructive themes as: "There are eight enemy helicopters in the sky; our victorious soldiers brought down six. How many are left?"

The Refugees

After the Vietnam War, more than two million people fled **Indochina**. Some **refugees** did not want to live in a **communist** country. Others hoped to escape the violence that continued in the region. After 1975, the Communist government in Cambodia killed several million of its own people. A few years later, Vietnam tried to replace Cambodian leader Pol Pot with a leader who would support its interests, leading to a war between the countries. In 1979, China invaded Vietnam, as punishment for the Vietnamese attack on Cambodia and Vietnam's harsh treatment of its Chinese residents. That war destroyed parts of Vietnam that had escaped major damage during the war with the U.S.

The first refugees were mostly former political and military leaders in South Vietnam. Over time, average citizens fled in greater numbers. Most refugees headed first for refugee camps in Thailand, the Philippines, Indonesia, and Hong Kong. From there, the majority went on to the U.S., Europe, and Australia. To help the refugees, the U.S. changed its immigration laws, making it easier for South-east Asians to enter the country. By the mid-1990s, more than 1.25 million refugees had settled in America. Occasionally, the Asian immigrants faced discrimination in their new homes. Many Americans feared the refugees would take away jobs from U.S. citizens or require large amounts of government aid. Over time, however, the fears over South-east Asian refugees have lessened, and many have prospered in America.

Many Vietnamese refugees left their country on small boats, and they were nicknamed "boat people." About 10 percent of the refugees died during their travels to a new home.

A survivor's letter

In 1979, Thanh-Hung fled Vietnam but was forced to return. In a letter he wrote to relatives who managed to leave Vietnam, he described his life at sea as one of the "boat people"—the name given to those who left by sea, often in unsuitable or overcrowded boats.

We floundered on the high seas for nineteen days and nights, and then our boat was carried by the currents back to Vietnamese territorial waters. We didn't know where we were. We ran aground at Phu Quy Island in the province of Phan Thiet. During those nineteen days and nights we had been tortured by hunger and thirst. Many had died. Others had committed suicide by jumping overboard when they had become delirious with thirst. Most of us had drunk our own urine. We had been robbed five times by Thai fishing boats, but we had nothing. It was because of these pirates that we had survived, because they gave us drinking water, and rice broth. Not all pirates were killers. It is thanks to them that I am alive to write this to you today.

During our escape, I cheated death at least twice. My dear brother and sister, our attempt to seek freedom, to seek our family reunion, to look for a better future at the end, achieved nothing. Now, back in Vietnam, I have lost everyone and everything . . . My dear brother and sister, why did our maker punish me by giving me such misery?

These Vietnamese-American students are part of the large refugee population that settled in California and other states after the war.

Vietnam Today

With its victory in 1975, Vietnam accomplished two major goals: independence and unity. The effects of the war, however, endure.

The economy is a major issue. The war destroyed industries and killed many young people who would have added to the country's wealth. Vietnam also faced U.S. sanctions (restrictions on the goods Americans could buy from or sell to Vietnamese). These sanctions, which were not lifted until 1994, limited the growth of some Vietnamese industries. During the 1980s, the government began adopting some **capitalist** methods to strengthen the economy. In the mid-1990s Vietnam was caught up in the financial crisis that hit many Asian countries and the government, under the control of the **Communist** Party, lost confidence in this approach. Now, some cities, particularly in the south, bustle with activity and the country exports some goods, but about one-third of the Vietnamese still live in poverty.

Vietnam also faces the long-term effects of U.S. weapons. The chemicals in **defoliants** such as Agent Orange are believed to have caused a high number of birth defects and other health problems. (Some U.S. soldiers claim their health, too, was damaged by the defoliants.) The Vietnamese also face continuing danger from unexploded landmines set during the war.

In 1995, Vietnam and the U.S. established official relations for the first time. Several years later, the U.S. signed a trade treaty with the Vietnamese, who hoped the deal would continue economic growth. The country faces many years of hard work to help all its citizens prosper.

A Vietnamese mother holds her daughter, who suffers from birth defects possibly related to her father's exposure to Agent Orange during the war. Up to one million Vietnamese may have suffered from the effects of dioxin, a chemical in that defoliant.

A poet's perception

Pham Tien Duat, a Vietnamese poet, fought for North Vietnam during the war. In 1997, he offered some of his thoughts on how his people cope with their memories of the conflict.

The women, too, want to put the war behind them, to forget it but they can't. How can those hundreds of thousands of wives forget when their husbands were killed before they could ever have their first child, and now live the rest of their still young lives as widows? How can those thousands of children born deformed at birth forget? How can thousands of invalid veterans forget?

Modern-day Saigon has been renamed Ho Chi Minh City and commuters jam the busy streets instead of fleeing **refugees**.

And yet, to open a new and bright chapter between the U.S. and Vietnam, it seems best if both sides close the door of the past. And rightly so, for hatred is neither good for others, nor for oneself. That sorrowful door to the past needs to be shut. But, in order to close a door, it's worthwhile to understand what it is that we close. Sadly, after over twenty years have passed since the war ended, many can still only vaguely see the contour of that door as if looking through a veil of mist.

I . . . have tried to write about the war, to describe and analyze it, but it still doesn't seem enough. It is as if I were standing in the midst of a crowd and calling out, but the noise makes it impossible for my friends to hear. There is therefore no choice but to call out once again, even if the voice becomes hoarse, until it is heard.

What Have We Learned?

Through the words of both soldiers and civilians, this book has tried to show the reality of the Vietnam War—or wars. The Vietnamese actually fought two wars to win their independence, a 30-year struggle that cost several million lives. The U.S. government played a key role from the beginning, hoping to stop the spread of **communism.** In the process, it supported a **corrupt** South Vietnamese government and lied to its own citizens. Many Americans felt betrayed, and their trust in their leaders was slow to return.

The North Vietnamese often said they would fight for years, if necessary, since they were fighting for their homeland. With their victory, they secured their communist rule in the south. Today, however, some Vietnamese—inside and out of the country—complain about the lack of **democracy** and freedom in Vietnam.

The Vietnam War had many lasting effects on both the victors and the defeated. Soldiers on both sides were crippled, and the war forced both sides to spend money on weapons that could have been used in other ways. In general, however, the civilians of Vietnam paid the highest price in casualties, while the survivors watched their homes and land destroyed.

The war also affected the spirit of both Vietnamese and Americans. U.S. leaders decided that in the future, its military would not fight distant wars unless the U.S. had a clear interest at stake, and it was sure it could win. The Vietnam experience has sometimes caused American leaders to avoid sending troops to foreign nations or to do so reluctantly, as when war broke out in Yugoslavia during the 1990s. Yet when they do, some Americans say the government is repeating the mistakes of Vietnam, as some critics charged when the U.S. invaded Iraq in 2003. For the Vietnamese, the war restored their pride as an independent nation. Now, the two countries, once such bitter enemies, find ways to work together for the future.

A bombed out guard tower, along with other remnants of the war, remind the Vietnamese of their long struggle for independence.

War memories

With improving relations between Vietnam and the United States, many U.S. soldiers have visited their old battlefields. Michael Austin wrote about his 1993 trip for a website dedicated to memories of the war.

Next day, we traveled north to Hue. I was surprised how the Citadel still bore the scars of **Tet** 1968. In fact, I almost expected to see a flak-jacketed Marine or sandal-clad **Viet Cong** jump from the dark recesses of a blown out building. Time had stood still in Vietnam, preserving one of the greatest battles of the war. Tru [Austin's guide] described the enemy's month-long occupation of the city, when thousands of Hue citizens were executed by the North Vietnamese for suspicion of being collaborators with the Saigon regime.

"They were shot, hung, hacked to death, burned or buried alive. Some were weighted down with stones and drowned in the river."

Technically a communist and my former enemy, Tru was also one of the most decent and understanding men I could hope to meet. That evening, we sat quietly at the edge of the Perfume River in Hue, sipping beer as we watched the sun set on the western mountains. Tru joined me in a toast to the six Blue Ghosts, all from the scout platoon, who were killed there June 11 and 12, 1972.

Timeline

1945   The Viet Minh, led by Ho Chi Minh, declare Vietnamese independence from France

1946   France bombards the city of Haiphong, triggering the first Vietnam War

1950   President Harry Truman begins direct aid to France to help it fight the Vietnamese

1954   With their victory at Dien Bien Phu, the Vietnamese win their war for independence; Vietnam is split in two along the **17th parallel**

1955   Ngo Dinh Diem takes control in South Vietnam

1959   North Vietnam begins armed revolt in the south, hoping to reunite Vietnam

1961   President John F. Kennedy increases the number of U.S. military advisors in South Vietnam from 900 to 3,000

1963   Diem is **assassinated** and replaced by a series of military leaders; Kennedy is assassinated and replaced by Lyndon Johnson; the number of U.S. military personnel in South Vietnam reaches 16,000

1964   Johnson uses a military incident in the Gulf of Tonkin to win approval from **Congress** for greater U.S. military action in **Indochina;** bombing of Ho Chi Minh Trail in Laos begins

1965   First heavy bombing of North Vietnam begins; first U.S. combat troops arrive in South Vietnam; Battle of Ia Drang is first major clash between Americans and North Vietnamese

1967   Major peace **demonstrations** across the United States; Nguyen Van Thieu becomes president of South Vietnam

1968   **Tet** Offensive; Johnson decides not to seek re-election; supporters of Richard Nixon play role in ending peace talks; Nixon is elected president; U.S. troops in Indochina reach more than 500,000

1969   Nixon begins Vietnamization policy and brings home first U.S. troops; bombing of Cambodia begins; My Lai Massacre takes place; Ho Chi Minh dies; more large anti-war protests in the United States

1970   Nixon sends ground troops into Cambodia; six college students die in anti-war protests

1971   Several newspapers publish the Pentagon Papers

1972   Nixon visits both China and the Soviet Union; the Watergate break-in occurs; Henry Kissinger and Le Duc Tho conduct peace talks in Paris; Nixon orders massive bombing of North Vietnam at Christmastime

1973   The U.S. and North Vietnam sign a peace treaty; U.S. POWs are released and last American troops pull out of South Vietnam, but the war continues; Nixon faces questions about his role in Watergate

1974   Congress cuts aid to South Vietnam; Nixon resigns

1975   North Vietnam wins the Vietnam War; **communist** governments also come to power in Cambodia and Laos; **refugees** begin fleeing the region

1982   The Vietnam Veterans Memorial opens in Washington, D.C.

1995   The United States and Vietnam establish official diplomatic relations

Further Reading

Downing, David. *Communism*. Chicago: Heinemann Library, 2003.

Downing, David. *John F. Kennedy*. Chicago: Heinemann Library, 2001.

Steele, Philip. *Ho Chi Minh*. Chicago: Heinemann Library, 2003.

Uschan, Michael V. *The Fall of Saigon: The End of the Vietnam War*. Chicago: Heinemann Library, 2002.

Willoughby, David. *The Vietnam War*. Chicago: Heinemann Library, 2001.

List of Primary Sources

The author and publisher gratefully acknowledge the following publications from which written sources in the book are drawn. In some cases the wording or sentence structure has been simplified to make the material more appropriate for a school readership.

p. 9: Vietnamese Declaration of Independence, printed in Robert J. McMahon (ed.), *Major Problems in the History of the Vietnam War*, (D.C. Heath and Company, 1990).

p. 11: Interview in *Vietnam: A Television History*, PBS TV Series, "Roots of a War" episode [available online at http://www.pbs.org/wgbh/amex/vietnam/101ts.html].

p. 13: John Foster Dulles speech to the Overseas Press Club, quoted in David Bender (ed.), *The Vietnam War: Opposing Viewpoints*, (Greenhaven Press, 1998).

p. 15: Interview "The Underground School" in Al Santoli, *To Bear Any Burden*. (E.P. Dutton, Inc., 1985).

p. 17: Homer Bigart, "A 'Very Real War' in Vietnam—and the Deep U.S. Commitment" in *Reporting Vietnam Part One: American Journalism 1959-1969*, (The Library of America, 1998).

p. 19: Interview in Robert Steinman, *The Soldiers' Story: Vietnam in Their Own Words*, (TV Books, 1999).

p. 21: Interview in Martha Hess, *Then the Americans Came: Voices from Vietnam*, (Four Walls/Eight Windows, 1993).

p. 23: Testimony from the Winter Soldier Investigation, as printed in the Congressional Record, April 7, 1971 and available online at the Sixties Project, http://lists.village.virginia.edu/sixties/HTML_docs/Resources/Primary.html.

p. 25: Le Ly Hayslip, with Jay Wurts, *When Heaven and Earth Changed Places: A Vietnamese Woman's Journey from War to Peace*, (Doubleday, 1989).

p. 27: Interview in David Chanoff and Doan Van Toai, *Portrait of the Enemy*, (Random House, 1986).

p. 29: Richard Pyle, "From Tonkin Gulf to Persian Gulf," CNN Cold War, available online at http://www.cnn.com/SPECIALS/cold.war/episodes/11/then.now.

p. 31: Ron Kovic, *Born on the Fourth of July*, (Pocket Books, 1976).

p. 33: Interview in Ron Steinman, *The Soldiers' Story*, (TV Books, 1999).

p. 35: Online chat with Hugh Thompson Jr., CNN Cold War, available at http://www.cnn.com/SPECIALS/cold.war/guides/debate/chats/thompson/

p. 37: Richard Nixon televised address, May 11, 1970, printed in Robert J. McMahon (ed.), *Major Problems in the History of the Vietnam War*, (D.C. Heath and Company, 1990).

p. 39: H. R. Haldeman, *The Haldeman Diaries: Inside the Nixon White House*, (G.P. Putnam's Sons, 1994).

p. 41: Henry Kissinger, *White House Years* (Little, Brown and Company, 1979).

pgs. 43 and 45: Interviews in Al Santoli, *To Bear Any Burden*, (E.P. Dutton, 1985).

p. 47: Letter printed in Lesleyanne Hawthorne (ed.). *Refugee: The Vietnamese Experience*, (Oxford University Press, 1982).

p. 49: Pham Tien Duat, "The Vietnam War: Remember in Order to Forget," at Vietnam Online, http://www.pbs.org/wgbh/amex/vietnam/reflect/duat.html.

p. 51: Mike Austin, "Closure: A Vietnam Story," Vietnam Veterans Homepage, available online at http://grunt.space.swri.edu/closure.htm.

Glossary

17th parallel line of latitude that served as the first border between North and South Vietnam

aggressors people who start military action against another group of people or country

ally state, organization, or person that supports another

ambush hide and launch a surprise attack

archive collection of documents, sources, or evidence

artillery large, mobile guns

assassination murder of a political figure

cadre highly trained and active member of a political party or military force

capitalism economic system that uses private wealth to produce goods and services

censor remove words or ideas from a news report

civil rights nonpolitical rights, such as freedom and equality, which belong to a person because he or she is a citizen, and regardless of race, religion, color, or sex

classified secret

Cold War period of East-West tension, 1946-1989, that stopped short of a hot (fighting) war

colonial relating to a colony, an area of land where political power and national resources are controlled by another country

communism political theory advocating a society in which all property and services are publicly owned and each person is paid and works according to his or her needs and abilities

Congress the highest law-making body of the United States

corrupt dishonest; open to bribery

court-martialled tried in a military court for an offense against military law

declassified formerly secret but now open

defoliant chemical that kills plants and trees

demilitarized zone area where weapons are not allowed

democratic practicing democracy, a system of government in the which the governed—the people—periodically choose their governors in free elections. Genuinely democratic states uphold human rights and freedoms.

demonstration large protest usually against a government or its policies, but sometimes in favor of them

diplomat someone representing one nation who talks to the representatives of another; not a military person

draft process for selecting troops to serve in the military

guerrilla war fighting style that relies on small unofficial forces that hide and then quickly strike an enemy

ideological relating to a set of basic beliefs that shape attitudes and actions

imperialism political and military system focused on taking over other countries or influencing their governments

Indochina part of South-east Asia that includes Cambodia, Laos, and Vietnam

napalm jelly-like form of gasoline that burns on contact

nationalism efforts to end foreign influence or control of one's homeland

nuclear weapon device that uses the energy inside atoms to create large explosions

press conferences meetings held by government officials to give information to news reporters

propaganda information spread by a country or organization to influence others' beliefs or actions in a specific way

refugee civilian who flees his or her home because of war or natural disasters

republic nation whose head of state is not a king or queen but a president

siege military tactic of surrounding enemy forces so they cannot move or easily obtain supplies

stockade simple prison or fort built out of wood

Tet Vietnamese New Year, celebrated in January or February

traumatic deeply disturbing

Viet Cong communist South Vietnamese guerilla fighters

West collective name for countries that share democratic political systems and capitalist economic systems; includes the U.S., Canada, and most of the countries of Europe

Appendix

Other nations that aided South Vietnam and the United States during the Vietnam War, as part of the Free World Military Forces:

Australia

New Zealand

The Philippines

South Korea

Taiwan (advisors only)

Thailand

In addition, more than 30 countries provided aid to South Vietnam, including Brazil, Canada, Israel, Japan, Pakistan, Turkey, and the United Kingdom.

Index